55 Creative Approaches For Challenging & Resistant Children & Adolescents

TECHNIQUES • ACTIVITIES • WORKSHEETS

Susan P. Epstein, LCSW

PESI
Publishing
& Media
www.pesipublishing.com

Copyright © 2014 by Susan Epstein, LCSW

Published by
PESI Publishing & Media
PESI, Inc
3839 White Ave
Eau Claire, WI 54703

Cover Design: Amy Rubenzer
Layout Design: Bookmasters
Edited by: Marietta Whittlesey

Printed in the United States of America

ISBN: 978-1-937661-27-4

PESI
Publishing
& Media
www.pesipublishing.com

Thank you to my husband, Michael, for your belief in me and support; to my parents, Naomi and Nathan Paulson, the most amazing role models a girl could ask for; and my children, Sarah and Daniel Rosenkrantz, the guinea pigs of my parenting experiments.

Table of Contents

Section I

Quick Tips for Rules and Boundaries

Section II

Quick Tips for Bonding and Connecting

Section III

Quick Tips for Problem Solving and Teachable Moments

Section IV

Quick Tips for Encouraging Calm, Respect, and Mindfulness

Section V

Quick Tips for Self- Regulation

Section VI

Quick Tips for Successful and Responsible Children

Section VII

Quick Tips for Engaging Kids in School and Learning

Section VIII

Quick Tips for a Happy, Healthy Home

About the Author

For more than 30 years, Susan Epstein has been a Licensed Clinical Social Worker, author, trainer, educator, and presenter. This is her second book with PESI Publishing and Media. Susan has also written and published four parenting books:

The Take Back Your Parenting Powers System, Are You Tired of Nagging? How to Get Cooperative Kids, Your Out-Of-Control Teen, and *The Little Book With A Lot of Attitude: A Guide to Parent-Teen Communication.* Susan also co-authored a children's book about death, loss, and healing titled *The Cat Who Lost Its Meow.*

She founded Parenting Powers in 2007 (www.ParentingPowers.com), a parent-coaching company that provides coaching, tele-classes, and in-home parent-coaching programs. In 2009, Susan partnered with Dr. Wayne Scott Andersen (NY Times Best Selling Author), leader and visionary with a goal to eradicate obesity in America. Susan is a Certified Health Coach through the Villanova University College of Nursing. She coaches clients, and trains and mentors health coaches all over the U.S. In 2013, Susan created and launched a virtual group coaching/supervision program for professionals working with challenging kids. Susan has been quoted as an expert in *Family Circle, Parents Magazine, American Baby Magazine,* and *New York Magazine,* along with regular radio and television appearances.

Introduction
A Letter to Parents and Caregivers

Agatha Christie once said, "I like living. I have sometimes been wildly, despairingly, acutely miserable, racked with sorrow, but through it all I still know quite certainly that just to be alive is a grand thing."

This quote reminds me of what it is like parenting on the rough days, the days when the kids don't listen, when your son or daughter is suspended from school, or when you find something you wish you hadn't found in your kid's room. These days are heart-wrenching, and they test us as parents.

How much patience do we have? How much grief and hardship must we endure? But even on the very worst days, we wouldn't trade our kids in or throw in the towel. We regroup and muster our strength; we are not sure how we do it, but we get up the next day determined to once again be the best parents we know how to be.

We do it, because we know that they need us. We do it because we are their best teachers. We do it because we love them and want them to grow up into good, productive, loving adults, who will do the same for their kids.

If you are like most parents, however, sometimes, you just don't know what to do or how to handle a given situation. If your child has been suspended from school, does that mean that you should also have a consequence at home, and if so, what should it be? How much? How harsh?

Remember, you are your child's best teacher. So when you do consequence, don't do it out of anger. Make it a teaching moment. Make it meaningful. Make it something your child will always remember.

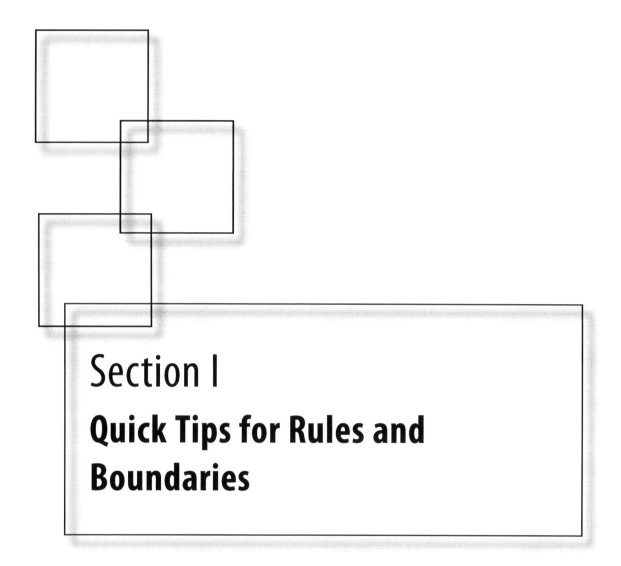

Section I
Quick Tips for Rules and Boundaries

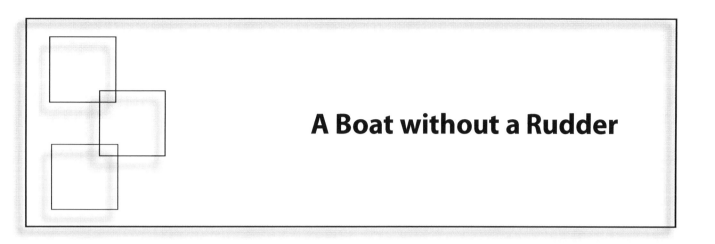

A Boat without a Rudder

Many parents and caregivers feel that they can never do enough to please their kids. The more they give, the more their kids beg for more.

As humans, we want to be "liked." We feel uncomfortable when someone is angry with us or gives us the cold shoulder. We will do anything to not be distanced from or in conflict with others. The problem with this and parenting is that it gets messy. The children's whining and complaining get to us and wears us down. Then we give in and let them have their way. Once you've fallen into this pattern, it's difficult to find your way out because, in an effort to get his or her way and to maintain the power, your child becomes even angrier than the last time.

When children become teens, it may seem as if they are closer to their friends than to their own family members, and this can feel hurtful. Remember, you want to be liked, and now they act as if they hate you! Some parents feel that they have to bend over backward to get any attention or to connect with their own kid.

This is where we as parents get into trouble. When parents want kids to like them, they might say yes when they really need to say no, or they might overlook it when they say, "Whatever," or roll their eyes. In an effort not to fight or make waves, parents give in over and over again. Remember the old saying "Give them an inch, and they'll take a yard"?

The real truth is that even if it seems that they are disconnecting from you and the family, children need boundaries and rules and want you to provide structure and set limits. Kids need direction, and if adults don't provide that, children are like boats without a rudders at sea.

Being a good parent can hurt or feel uncomfortable, but having your kid get in trouble in school or in the community hurts more.

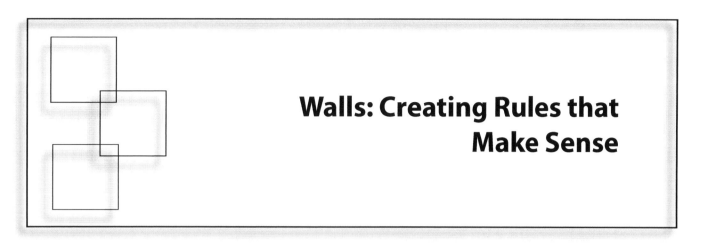

Walls: Creating Rules that Make Sense

Before I built a wall I'd ask to know what I was walling in or walling out.
— Robert Frost

PURPOSE

To define rules that are logical and reasonable and that provide a teachable moment, use the following questions to clarify the rules you currently have.

Common Questions and Complaints about Kids

Why won't my kids listen?

_____

Why do they break my rules?

_____

Why are they so disrespectful?

_____

Why are they so angry?

_____

Questions to Ask Instead

What are you asking them to do that they are not listening?

_____

What is the purpose of the rules you have created?

_____

How do you deal with disrespect?

_____

Why are you so angry?

_____

WORKSHEET: BEFORE I BUILD A WALL

If you have a rule, know why and if you are looking for a place start; develop these rules under these categories:

Ensuring Safety

1. (Example) "No texting while driving."

2. _____

3. _____

4. _____

5. _____

Teaching Manners

1. (Example) "When you want something use the word *please*."

2. _____

3. _____

4. _____

5. _____

Teaching Consideration

1. (Example) "Call me if you are going to be past your curfew."

2. _____

3. _____

4. _____

5. _____

Take the Gentle Path

PURPOSE

To help parents and caregivers learn how to take the gentle path. By doing so, you will be able to avoid power struggles and the guilt and regret that often follows.

How to Do It Differently

Power struggles—we've all been in them, we've started them, and we've been sucked into them; then something so simple becomes a tornado, and it's hard to even remember how we got there.

If you find yourself being pulled into a power struggle with your child, take a deep breath and start a robotic delivery of your expectations:

You will not talk to me that way.

or

It's okay if you don't finish dinner, but the kitchen is closed till 7 tomorrow morning. Your choice." (And stick with it by repeating this sentence until your kid stops fighting with you.)

Remember, don't let the child see you upset and out of control. Stay calm and take the gentle path.

In session with parents/caregivers, go through the worksheet on page 8, "Understanding Power Struggles," to identify what triggers are causing battles at home. Take this one step further to problem-solve each of the areas.

WORKSHEET: UNDERSTANDING POWER STRUGGLES

Let's look at your current situation. Answer the following questions about power struggles you've been a part of.

Questions

1. What power struggles do you have?

_____
_____
_____
_____

2. What time of day do these power struggles happen?

_____
_____
_____
_____

3. Who is involved?

_____
_____
_____
_____

4. Are the power struggles around things you want your child to do or around things you want your child to stop doing?

_____
_____
_____
_____

5. How important is it that one of you wins?

_____
_____
_____
_____

6. How do you feel at the end of the struggle?

_____
_____
_____
_____

Best Friend, Archenemy? What Type of Parent Are You?

PURPOSE

To learn about your parenting style and to offer an opportunity to have a closer, more rewarding relationship with your children and adolescents.

If you are having trouble with your kids or are trying to co-parent and it isn't working well, the style of parenting you are using may be why. Take the following Parent Quiz.

Parent Quiz

Rate the following on a scale of 1 to 3 as to whether it represents your style of parenting:

1. All the time
2. Sometimes
3. Never

"My child is my best friend! All his or her friends love me because I really understand them. They love coming over here because I give them a lot of freedom and space." (However, sometimes I wonder if I am too lenient and too permissive.)

Parents are usually fearful of their kids. They are afraid to say no because their child won't like them. _____

"My child is my 'archenemy.' He or she says that he or she hates me and that I don't get him or her, and he or she is either in his or her room or at a friend's house. I don't know anything about his or her life." (Am I too hard on my child? He or she is always in trouble with us, and we are all miserable.)

Archenemy parents are very strict and often over punish and over consequence. They are afraid that their child will grow up and be a really, really bad person. _____

The thing that both of these types of parents have in common is *guilt*.

Try the following to gain a balanced relationship with your child:

- Forget about being best friends with your child, but do get to know their friends and the parents of their friends.

- Do let your son or daughter have friends over. Give your child space, but be around and aware. Have a set of rules of which you both are aware. Make the consequences for failing to obey these rules available.

- Draw up a contract/agreement of what is expected and what will result if the contract is broken.

- Hold your child accountable for respectful behavior, and correct every time him or her when you notice.

- Remain interested in your child's life, but let him or her have a life—don't smother him or her.

And aim for this:

For the most part, I know what is going on in my kid's life. I know most of his or her friends, and my kid respects most of my rules most of the time.

I Want to Stop Nagging

PURPOSE

To help you identify how **"nagging"** isn't helping your child or children cooperate and to lay the foundation for the introduction of motivation, systems, and games to engage kids to cooperate.

List the things you want to have your child or children to do (e.g., pick up toys, go to bed without a fuss, chores). Remember, this is *not* a list of the things you want your child to *stop* doing. A great way to compile this list is to keep it with you during the week, and every time you ask your child to do something and it doesn't get done, or you have to remind him or her, or you feel like screaming, add that item to this list.

1. _____

2. _____

3. _____

4. _____

5. _____

6. _____

7. _____

8. _____

9. _____

10. _____

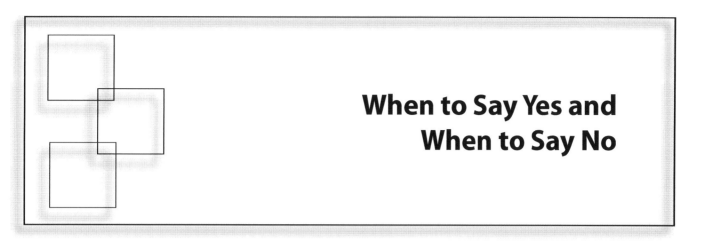

When to Say Yes and When to Say No

PURPOSE

To help you clarify why you respond in a certain way to children and adolescents.

When kids ask permission to do something, whether it's to stay up late, play one more game or not participate in family life; sometimes, adults don't think through their responses setting them up for tantrums, meltdowns and chaos.

Use the following to identify situation in which you may not have thought through situations before saying yes or no. For example,

By saying "YES" to staying up past bedtime, I am saying "NO" to a smooth, calm morning.

By saying "NO" to my teen being unsupervised after school, I am saying "YES" to ensuring that my teen won't make risky and unsafe choices.

Saying "YES" . . . Saying "NO"

1. By saying "YES" to _____,
   I am saying "NO" to _____.

2. By saying "YES" to _____,
   I am saying "NO" to _____.

3. By saying "YES" to _____,
   I am saying "NO" to _____.

4. By saying "YES" to _____,
   I am saying "NO" to _____.

5. By saying "YES" to _____,
   I am saying "NO" to _____.

Saying "NO" . . . Saying "YES"

1. By saying "NO" to _____,

   I am saying "YES" to _____.

2. By saying "NO" to _____,

   I am saying "YES" to _____.

3. By saying "NO" to _____,

   I am saying "YES" to _____.

4. By saying "NO" to _____,

   I am saying "YES" to _____.

5. By saying "NO" to _____,

   I am saying "YES" to _____.

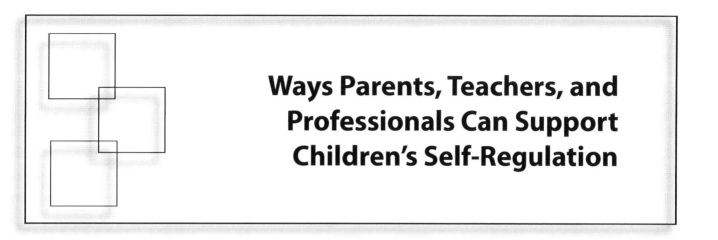

Ways Parents, Teachers, and Professionals Can Support Children's Self-Regulation

PURPOSE

In order for a positive change to occur, children need reinforcement in all their environments (especially school and home). Therapists can assist in the process by sharing these supportive questions and statements.

Prompts

- You seem upset. Would you like your Cool Down Kit?
- Do you think using the Breathing Square would help you calm down?
- Would you like your cue cards for Stop, Breathe, Reflect & Choose?
- Would you like to play a game or read a book during your free time?
- Remember that if you finish your math problems, you'll be able to go outside for recess with other kids.

Reinforcing

- I love the way you are sitting still and eating your dinner.
- That was so nice of you to help your sister with her homework.
- I am so proud of the way you behaved in the supermarket.
- Wow! You stayed in your bed for 30 minutes without getting up!
- Thank you so much for saying "please."

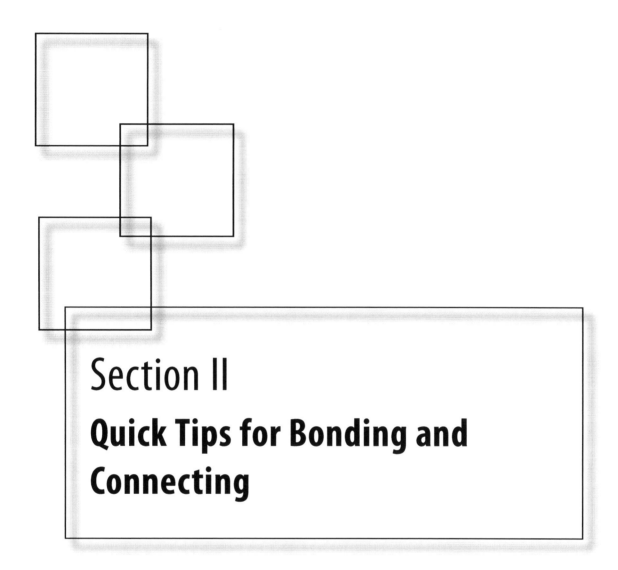

Section II
Quick Tips for Bonding and Connecting

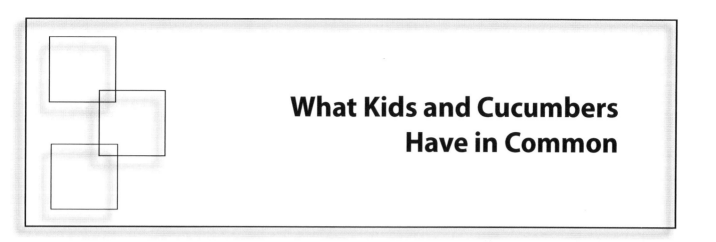

What Kids and Cucumbers Have in Common

A few years ago, I planted a vegetable garden with lettuce, pole beans, tomatoes, cucumbers, and herbs. Every day I went outside to check it. For weeks very little happened. Then one morning I went out to check again. I couldn't believe my eyes! The tomatoes were three times larger than they were the day before, the lettuce had doubled in size, and the cucumbers had these really cool shoots coming out of them that had actually attached to the fencing and had wrapped around it several times to hold on. My garden had exploded with activity, and it seemed to have happened overnight.

The magic in my garden made me think about my own kids. They used to be little and then one day and I can't tell you when; like the shoots of the cucumbers, they were taller than me, were independent, had parts of their lives that didn't include me and then transformed into grown-ups.

The minutes, hours, days, months, and years flew by in a flash. I have photos documenting that the time spent together actually happened. I remember some of it in bits and pieces, and then some of it is a complete blur.

Looking back, I know that I had spent time looking in their eyes, talking to them, and creating memories every chance I could. What I have today is a wonderful, close relationship with both of them.

You've heard it over and over: "Enjoy them now because when you least expect it, in a blink of an eye, they'll be adults and on their own."

Start by looking into your kids eyes five times a day. Don't take your eyes off them. Maybe, just maybe, you'll see the magic happening right in front of you.

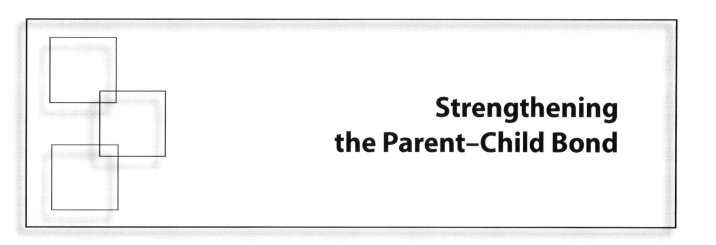

Strengthening the Parent–Child Bond

PURPOSE

To assist parents/caregivers in family therapy with bonding with their kids no matter what age

Fill out the following worksheet with the client to help them develop and strengthen their bond with their child.

1. I Love You

Tell your child daily that you love him or her—no matter his or her age. Even on trying days or after a parent–child disagreement, when you don't exactly "like" your child at that moment, it is more important than ever to express your love. A simple "I love you" goes a long way toward developing and then strengthening a relationship.

These are the times of day I will tell my child I love them (e.g., before he or she leaves for school, when he or she comes home, and before bed): _____ ___

_____

2. Teach Your Values and Beliefs

Tell your child what you believe and why. Allow time for your child to ask questions and answer them honestly. Reinforce these teachings often.

The following are my basic values and beliefs: _____

_____

3. Create a Special Name Or Code Word

Create a special name for your child or a secret code word with your child that is positive and special that you can use between each other. Use this name as a simple reinforcement of your love. The code word can be established to have special meaning between your child and you that only you two understand.

Our secret code word is _____

_____

4. A Special Bedtime Ritual
For younger children, reading a favorite bedtime book or telling stories is a ritual that will be remembered most likely throughout their life. It's key to have a ritual with teens, too!

Our bedtime ritual is _____

_____

5. Let Your Children Help You
Parents sometimes inadvertently miss out on opportunities to forge closer relationships by not allowing their child to help them with various tasks and chores. Be prepared if they say no. Not the same as the nonnegotiable chore that's been assigned to them.

I ask my children to help me with the following _____.

6. Play with Your Child
The key is to really play with your child. You really are your child's favorite toy! Ask him or her, "Can I play with you?" "Want to play a video game?" or "Want to play a game of Uno?"

I will ask my child to play with me during these times of the day _____

_____

7. Eat Meals as a Family
Families who eat together have better relationships. It gives you a forum for conversation. Be careful to be positive at dinner time. It's not the time for discipline

Our family will eat the following meals together: _____

_____

8. Seek Out One-On-One Opportunities Often
Make time to spend one-on-one time with your child; if you have more than one child, allot time to spend with each. Even if it's just for 30 minutes, it counts. You could do an outing two times a month with just one of your children.

I will spend one on one time with each of my children in this way: _____

_____

9. Respect Your Child's Choices
Let your child dress him- or herself, and let your child be creative with his or her hairstyle and choices of colors as long as it is appropriate. It does not reflect on you if your child is wearing plaid and stripes. In fact, you might be raising a creative designer!

I will respect my child in the following ways: _____

_____

10. Make Them Number One
Even when your life is stressed out make sure that you do steps 1 through 9. You are creating memories with your child, and who doesn't want to look back on his or her childhood and know how loved and important he or she was to his or her parents?

_____

_____

Who's Got Your Back?

Are you upset, little friend? Have you been lying awake worrying? Well,
don't worry . . . I'm here. The flood waters will recede, the famine will end,
the sun will shine tomorrow, and I will always be here to take care of you.

– Charlie Brown to Snoopy

PURPOSE

Use this with adolescents to help them identify the people who support them in their lives.

Who has your back? Who will be there for you? If you don't have a support system, feeling all alone can be very overwhelming.

Having a support system is especially important if you are creating change in your life. Making a commitment to improve is a giant step. Most of us have the best intentions, start out full force, and then kaput! It's over and done, and we feel like a failure. The reason? Lack of support. One of the most important discoveries I have made in the past 10 years is that Support = Success. Every endeavor I have made in business or in my personal life has been filled with supportive friends, mentors, and the people who love me and I love back.

Use the worksheet "Who's Got Your Back?" with teens in the session to assist them in identifying their current support system, and then brainstorm additional people they can add to their support system.

WORKSHEET: WHO'S GOT YOUR BACK?

Make of a list of the people in your life who you can count on. If you come up short, make another list of potential new people to cultivate relationships with. Then reach out and connect.

People who support me:

1. _____

_____

2. _____

_____

3. _____

_____

4. _____

_____

5. _____

_____

People who potentially would support me:

1. _____

_____

2. _____

_____

3. _____

_____

4. _____

_____

5. _____

_____

Creating Memories for Life

PURPOSE

Create rituals and structure that provide children and adolescents positive childhood memories; this can be presented in family therapy sessions

MATERIALS

Timer, Creating Memories worksheet, pens

Any time is a great time to put into place family rituals, things that you do over and over again. It could be that you eat outdoors or that you take a walk together after dinner. It might be that you go camping or take some type of family vacation together or visit relatives. It doesn't matter what you do or if it costs money or is free—what matters most is the *time* together. This is fairly easy to make happen with some children, but how do you entice children with special needs and 'tweens and teens to participate in family time?

During your family meeting brainstorm things that your child want to do and enjoy doing. Challenge him or her to come up with at least twenty-five ideas. You can even use a timer to make it fun. Let your child know that some activities can cost but that you want him or her to think of as many ideas as possible that are free. You can give ideas, such as playing a game on Friday nights after dinner or making a home movie with your phone.

As you brainstorm with your child, be conscious of his or her developmental stage. This is meant to be fun and not a setup for you and your child to become frustrated or to have a meltdown. If his or her behavior gets out of control, make an effort to correct and teach rather than punish or send the child out of the room.

Here are a few suggestions to get your creative juices flowing:

- Set the table with a cloth and your best dishes once a week and make a certain element of the meal the same (favorite dessert, special meal, etc.).
- During summer, once a week take a picnic to the park or beach for dinner.

- During winter, set one night a week aside as family movie night.
- On Sunday mornings, sleep a bit later and have brunch together.
- Take pictures of the table set, the picnic, all the activities that you do together.

Do these same activities over and over again year in and year out, and you have created wonderful family memories for you and your kids.

Use the following worksheet on page 27, "Creating Memories," with parents/caregivers or the entire family during a session. Then ask them to pick two or three to implement during the following week.

WORKSHEET: CREATING MEMORIES

Summer Memories: Fun Things to Do as a Family

1. _____

2. _____

3. _____

4. _____

5. _____

Family Night Memories (Games, Favorite Foods, Movies)

1. _____

2. _____

3. _____

4. _____

5. _____

Dinnertime Memories (Cooking Together, Candlelight on the Table (if safe!), Sunday Dinner)

1. _____

2. _____

3. _____

4. _____

5. _____

Other Memories to Create

1. _____

2. _____

3. _____

4. _____

5. _____

Look at Me!

PURPOSE

To increase eye contact in children with Opposition Defiant Disorder, Attention Deficit Hyperactivity Disorder, and/or Autism Spectrum Disorder.

MATERIALS

Timer, stickers, paper, pen

Tell the child or adolescent that you are going to play the staring game. After each exercise, log his or her responses on the following worksheet on page 30.

1. Set the timer and see who can stare the longest (most people can't stare beyond 5 seconds). Stop and ask, "What was that like?" Have the child record his or her comfort level on the worksheet.

2. Place a small sticker between your eyes and ask the child to look at that. Stop and ask, "What was that like?" Have the child record his or her comfort level on the worksheet.

3. Next, try the triangle approach: Look at one eye for 5 seconds, the second eye for 5 seconds, and the mouth for 5 seconds. Stop and ask: "What was that like?" Have the child record his or her comfort level on the worksheet.

WORKSHEET: LOOK AT ME

On a scale of 1 to 3, indicate your level of comfort:

1. Okay

2. Uncomfortable

3. Very Uncomfortable

Exercise 1	
Exercise 2	
Exercise 3	
Exercise 4	
Exercise 5	
Exercise 6	
Exercise 7	
Exercise 8	
Exercise 9	
Exercise 10	

Exercise 1	
Exercise 2	
Exercise 3	
Exercise 4	
Exercise 5	
Exercise 6	
Exercise 7	
Exercise 8	
Exercise 9	
Exercise 10	

Continuing practicing!

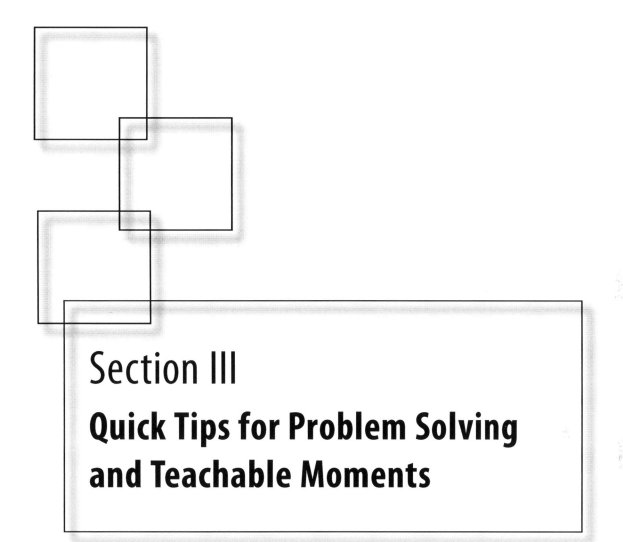

Section III

Quick Tips for Problem Solving and Teachable Moments

Miss-Takes! New Takes!

PURPOSE

Mistakes are a part of life, and teaching children to handle them in positive ways encourages children to take personal responsibility and promotes learning.

Think of a mistake as a *miss*-take! You interpreted the situation incorrectly, and you made a choice to do something or behave in a certain way. Using the following three steps, work with children to make their miss-takes into new takes.

New Takes!

1. See it—"I made a mistake."

2. Say it—"I'm sorry."

3. Solve it—"Let's work on a solution together."

The first two steps—"See it" and "Say it"—encourage mindfulness and connection. The third step teaches learning through making a mistake and focuses on the teachable moment rather than the typical "shaming." It is crucial to go through all three in this order for the teachable moment and to lock in the learning.

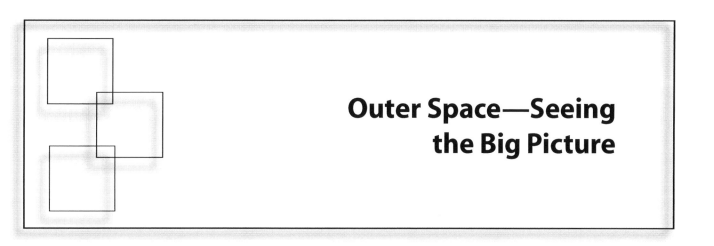

Outer Space—Seeing the Big Picture

PURPOSE

To encourage children to pull back and see their problems from the meta-view rather than being caught up in the small stuff. This is especially helpful for kids with obsessive compulsive disorder.

Tell the child that you are going on a trip into outer space. Ask him or her to close his or her eyes and read the following script:

Please fasten your seatbelt and get ready for the trip. In a few moments we are going to take off and travel way into outer space. OK, here we go, get ready—blast off!

We are traveling fast. As you look out your window you can see your house, now your street, now your city, and now the outline of your state. Now you can see water and the coastline. We just broke through the clouds and now through the Milky Way Galaxy.

Let's float here for a while and look at all the pretty stars and looking down there is planet Earth. Take out your special binoculars and see us in this room. We are going to look at your problem from way up here.

What do you notice? How tiny are you? Me? The universe is so big. Let's talk about your problem from up here. What can you tell yourself about your problem when viewing it at this distance?

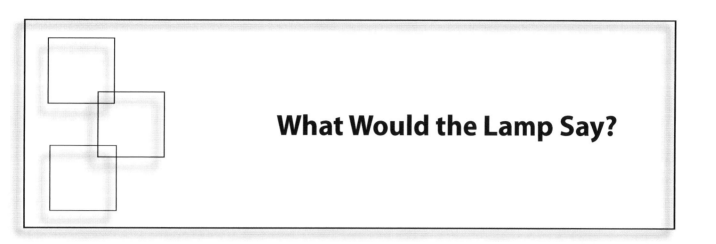

What Would the Lamp Say?

PURPOSE

To elicit a different perspective from a teen to aid in problem solving. Note that this activity is recommended for children 12 years old and older.

Use this activity when you, as a therapist, have worked with teen on coping strategies to help improve the situation but nothing seems to be working and the teen is becoming more frustrated.

For example, when a teen says, "I have no friends," try this:

1. Ask the teen to look around the room and name at least 10 objects such as a lamp, desk, book, mug, calendar, and so on.

2. The therapist should write these down on the worksheet as the teen dictates (see following page).

3. Now ask the teen to share what each of these objects would say about the problem or issue. It has to be from the perspective of that object using metaphor. If the teen has difficulty understanding the concept offer a few examples to model the exercise; for example,

   The lamp says, "We have to shed more light on the problem."
   The book says, "We need more information, keep looking deeper."
   The calendar says, "Let's look at how long you've had this problem."

Use these prompts in the worksheet on page 38 to create more conversation and dig deeper into solving the problem.

WORKSHEET: WHAT WOULD THE LAMP SAY?

List the objects in the room and what they would say about the problem:

1. _____

The _____ says, _____

_____

_____

2. _____

The _____ says, _____

_____

_____

3. _____

The _____ says, _____

_____

_____

4. _____

The _____ says, _____

_____

_____

5. _____

The _____ says, _____

_____

_____

Random Act of Kindness Wall

PURPOSE

To encourage empathy, compassion, and good deeds in a group setting

MATERIALS

A space on a wall or big bulletin board; pens, pencils, and/or markers; paper cutouts of happy face or doves (see following page); and push pins and/or tape

Tell the children that whenever they notice someone in the family or in the group doing something for another person or being kind, they are to take one of the cutouts and write the other person's name on it and the nice deed they did. For example, Susie helped Sarah pick up her backpack when it fell off the chair.

Then tape or pin the cutout to the Kindness Wall for all to see.

Have a Random Acts of Kindness Week or Month and challenge the kids to see how many cutouts they can put on the wall. At the end of the event, celebrate by reading all the cutouts aloud and have a little party with surprises and treats to celebrate all the kindness in your home or classroom.

By focusing children's attention on the type of behavior you want from them, you will notice a decrease in the type of behavior you want less of!

Make 5 to 10 copies of the worksheet on the following page, and then let the child cut out the images for the Random Acts of Kindness board.

Copy these pictures onto cardstock or heavy-weight paper and let the kids cut them out.

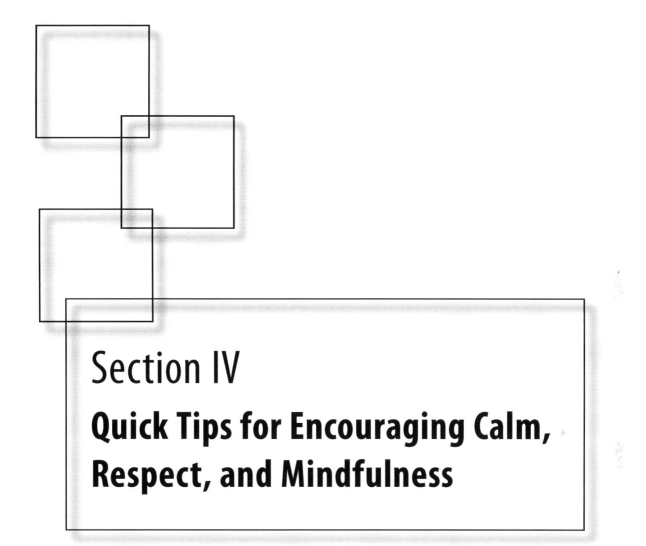

Section IV
Quick Tips for Encouraging Calm, Respect, and Mindfulness

Meta-View

Although my kids are grown, they are still my "kids." When we get together, it's funny how I see some of the same behaviors, traits, and interactions that were present when they were children. I am watching this all from a meta-view and super conscious of my triggers and reactions. I am continually reminded of my own part in our relationship and that they are people in their own right with their own lives. About children, Kahil Gibran wrote in his book, *The Prophet*, "They come from you but they are not you."

When children are frustrated, shutdown, angry, or disrespectful, try this:

- Listen to children.

- Watch for your triggers when they say or do something.

- Correct with love and guidance.

- Treat the children with the respect that you would like from them.

Great Job! Breaking away from Negativity

PURPOSE

To encourage empathy and compassion in children and adolescents; this activity can be practiced with parents during family therapy sessions.

Children are often awarded negative attention: getting scolded for doing things they shouldn't be doing. This often backfires and turns into huge battles of the will. The following are examples:

"Stop hitting your brother!

"You are so rude!"

"Learn some manners!"

Instead of correcting through lecturing, start by noticing and complimenting kids whenever they do something right or comply with your request. The following is an example:

Mom: "Mary, please turn off the TV now and come to dinner."

Mary: "Okay, Mom." Mary turns off the TV and goes to dinner table.

Mom: "Thank you, Mary. I really love when you listen to me the first time. Great job!"

Second, take notice whenever your child does a chore or something else required of him or her:

Teacher: "Josh, you've been able to sit still today and complete your math problems. Great job!

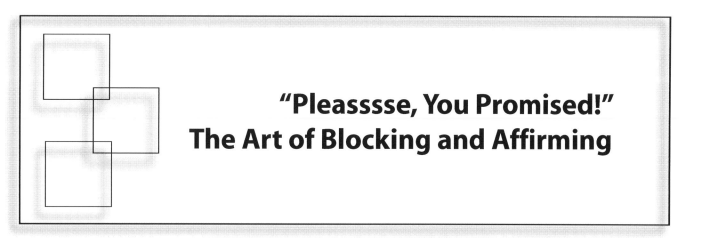

"Pleasssse, You Promised!"
The Art of Blocking and Affirming

PURPOSE

To reduce conflicts and power struggles struggles between parents and kids and teachers and students

We often knee-jerk react to our kids' negative behaviors and within a split second our homes and classrooms turn into a battleground. An hour later, we are kicking ourselves, wondering why we didn't act calmly and use our robot voices.

Every parent/caregiver wants to make sure his or her kid gets it—whatever the "it" of the day is. Here are some common ways adults try to get their point across:

- **Explaining the same thing again and again:** "No, you can't have a cell phone. You are not old enough, and it's too much money, and you'll probably lose it . . . blah . . . blah . . . blah . . ."

- **Lecturing:** "Don't keep asking me for the cell phone. I told you the reasons why. You are getting on my nerves, and I need some peace and quiet around here."

- **Questioning:** "How many times have I told you no about the cell phone? I'm not discussing it anymore. How come you don't get *no* when I say no?"

- **Negotiating:** "Maybe if you are good all weekend, I'll think about it."

- **Yelling:** "I told you not to bring that up again!"

- **Ignoring:** Shutting down and not speaking to the child.

- **Sending away:** "Go to your room!"

Kids know what our automatic responses will be, and they are overly prepared for the comeback:

- **Begging:** "*Pleeeeeease!*"

- **Challenging:** "You promised!"

- **Crying:** "Everyone else has one."

- **Tuning out:** "La,da, La,da"

- **Guilt:** "I hate you! You are mean!"

The following are approaches that work for affirming:

- **Robotic approaches:** Repeat, "This is not up for discussion," calmly until your child stops.

- **Listen and affirm:** "I know that this is important to you, but the answer is no."

- **Follow:** If your child walks away, follow him or her, get him or her to look at you, and then say, "Do not walk away from me. It is disrespectful."

- **Don't send away and don't leave:** Stick it out. Your sending a child away or your leaving feels like rejection and banishment to a kid. Stay with your child like Velcro until he or she stops.

It does take a bit of energy up front to put on the calm face. But in the long run, you will save energy and will avoid power struggles, tantrums, meltdowns, and slammed doors.

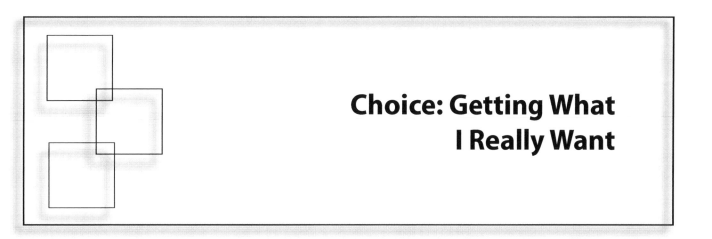

Choice: Getting What I Really Want

PURPOSE

To help children make choices that give them the outcome that they truly want

The following is a script uses a boy who regularly hits his brother and is sent to his room as an example of how the process works. Use this to encourage children to see how their behavior sometimes gets them the complete opposite of what they want. Offer the child help in getting what he or she wants by problem solving and brainstorming ways that don't result in negative behaviors and in consequences that he or she doesn't like or want.

> Therapist: "Do you like being sent to your room?"
>
> Child: "No!"
>
> Therapist: "If you didn't hit your brother, would you be sent to your room?"
>
> Child: "Nope."
>
> Therapist: "Why do you hit your brother?"
>
> Child: "I want him to play with me."
>
> Therapist: "When you hit your brother, does he play with you?
>
> Child: "No, I get in trouble."
>
> Therapist: "Right and you get sent to your room."
>
> Child: "Yes."
>
> Therapist: "Would you like me to help you get to play with your brother and not get sent to your room?"
>
> Child: "Yes!"

Use the worksheet "Choices: Getting What I Want" on page 50 with the child to help him/her understand how their choices affect the outcome of what happens.

WORKSHEET: CHOICES: GETTING WHAT I WANT

The negative behavior was

_____

_____

_____

_____

The outcome of the behavior was

_____

_____

_____

_____

Is the child happy with the result?

_____

_____

_____

_____

What did the child want before exhibiting the negative behavior?

_____

_____

_____

_____

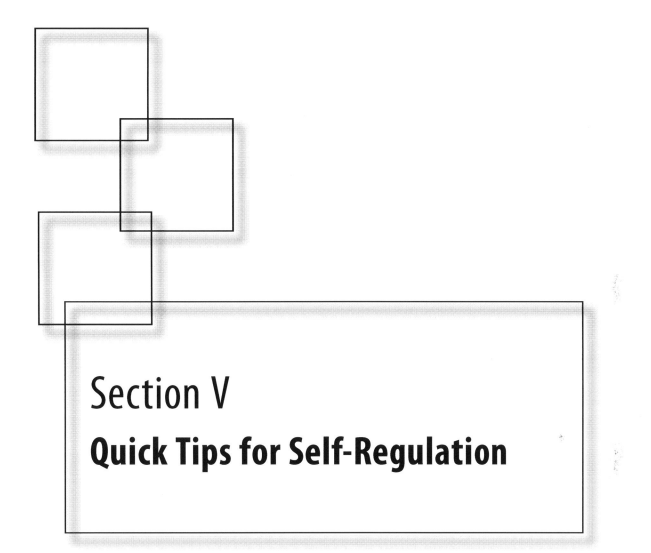

Section V
Quick Tips for Self-Regulation

Sometimes We Lose It

Over the years I've worked with many parents and teachers who come to me with a child or a teen who is out of control. The first meeting is usually like this: "My child doesn't listen," "My child has tantrums," "My child is disrespectful," "My child hit me," and so on.

I ask them about their communication style. "Well, I interrupt my child. I scream and yell. Sometimes I say things I regret; sometimes I lose it." I'll admit that staying in your robot is hard work. Adults have many emotional hot buttons that when pushed, can drive them nuts, and they are calling at us, coaxing us, to scream, yell, cry and stamp our own feet.

Some kids are difficult most of the time, and it takes lots of patience not to lose your cool. Other kids are fine most of the time, and then *boom*—like a time bomb, they explode and stop cooperating. Why, why, why, can't they just behave?

Here's why: They are little humans. They have good days and bad days just like us. When was the last time that you didn't get frustrated at work, or while being on hold with the insurance company, or while waiting all day for the delivery that never comes, or while waiting by the side of the road for assistance when your vehicle has broken down?

As adults, for the most part, we have learned to modulate our emotions and keep them in check. We have learned not to kick the police officer and scream at the nice tech person we've been on the phone with for two hours while our computer continues to crash.

Sometimes, we even procrastinate, put things off, get distracted—we skip washing our faces or brushing our teeth before we go to bed, stay up too late, and break the rules. Sometimes—yes, it's true—we have temper tantrums right in front of our kids!

So the next time your child

- talks back;
- whines;
- begs;
- hits or kicks;
- spits or bites;
- throws a tantrum;

- swears;

- threatens to leave, run away, or live with another parent/caregiver;

- ignores you or walks away;

- throws or breaks things;

- intimidates you;

- becomes melodramatic;

- tries to guilt trip you; and/or

- leaves you out of the loop,

remember that it is your job to teach him or her how to act, how to emote, and how to get his or her needs met. If you are patient and loving and understanding, your child will get it. If you melt down while they are, they will become confused.

A Watched Pot Never Boils!

PURPOSE

To help children monitor and identify feelings; this activity can be used in individual and family therapy.

Discuss how feelings can be mild and intense. Use the metaphor of a pot on the stove to teach the child the varying levels of emotions involved in being angry.

Date	Feeling	Watch	Steam	Boils
EX: 2/12	MAD			X

Send the activity worksheet (see the following page) home with the parent/caregiver and ask him or her to monitor meltdowns and explosions for one week.

WORKSHEET: A WATCHED POT

Monitor your child's meltdowns and feelings and the intensity of those feelings.

Date	Feeling	Watch	Steam	Boils

Calming Cards

PURPOSE

To help children create images that remind them that they can choose to do an activity to get to a calm and happy place

Copy the images shown and cut them out, or you create your own images. Keep these in the "Cool Down Kit." Ask the child to help you create the list specifically for him or her using the worksheet on the following page.

WORKSHEET: ACTIVITIES I CAN DO TO CALM DOWN

Use this worksheet to brain storm ideas with kids before creating their own cards.

1. _____

2. _____

3. _____

4. _____

5. _____

6. _____

7. _____

8. _____

9. _____

10. _____

11. _____

12. _____

13. _____

14. _____

15. _____

16. _____

17. _____

Work with the child to transfer the child's favorite cool down ideas to these blank cards.

I Am Calm

I Am Calm

I Am Calm

The Feeling GPS, Part 1

PURPOSE

To encourage children to monitor their behavior and to help them make a choice about letting their feelings rule their behaviors; this activity can be used with children and with families.

Have children draw a map showing where their feeling car is going.

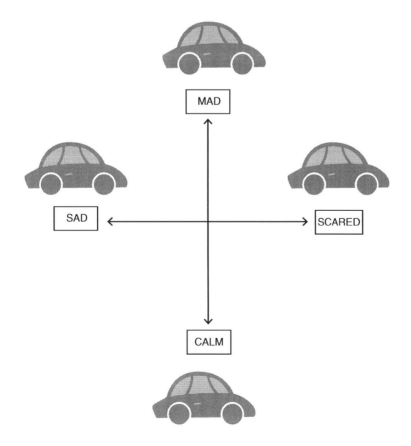

The Feelings GPS, Part 2:
Let's Drive to CALM

PURPOSE

To help children process the connection between their feelings, their behaviors, and the consequences of those choices

Explain to the child that sometimes feelings trigger kids to hit or take out their feelings on others. What happens to you?

For example, "When I go the MAD place I hit my brother and then my mom sends me to my room."

When I go to the MAD place this happens:

_____

When I go to the SCARED place this happens:

_____

When I go to the SAD place this happens:

_____

When I go to the CALM place this happens:

_____

Rag Doll

PURPOSE

To promote relaxation and self-regulation, and to calm down before bedtime for children ages 4 through 10

MATERIALS

The following script and a small stuffed animal

Read each set of directions slowly, using a calming tone in your voice. As children progress through this technique, they'll pay attention to each muscle group, taking note of the difference between tense muscles and relaxed muscles.

You can record this and add it to the Cool Down Kit.

Script

1. Lie down on your back and close your eyes. Breathe in deeply through your nose. (Pause and silently count to three). Now, let out your breath very slowly, as if you're giving a long sigh: *Ahhhhhh.*

   Be aware of the muscles in your face. Relax them, beginning with your jaw. Next, relax your shoulders; feel the tension melt away. Now, feel your tummy. Put your stuffed animal on your belly button and hold the stuffed animal in place. Put your other hand on top of that hand. Breathe in deeply and let out the breath slowly. Notice how your stuffed animal rises and falls. Let's make our animal rise and fall 10 times. (Repeat at least 10 times.)

2. Next, relax the muscles in your body. Pretend that you have an orange in your right hand. Squeeze as hard as you can and count to five: one, two, three, four, five. Good. Pay attention to the tension in your muscles. Now, drop the orange and let your muscles relax. (Repeat for the left hand.)

3. Now sit up and pretend you're a cat or a dog that's just woken up from a nap. Stretch your arms high above your head. Now, let your arms drop. Don't try to stop them. Just let them fall. See how good that feels? Now, reach for the ceiling. Stretch higher. Higher! Go as high as you can. Now let your arms drop to your side. Doesn't that feel good?

4. Now, let's work on your jaw muscles. We're going to pretend that you have a hard piece of candy in your mouth, and you're going to try as hard as you can to bite through it. Bite hard. Harder! Now, relax your jaw muscles. Let's try it again. (Repeat.) Now, relax. Pretend you are swallowing the candy. Yum! Feel the tension melt away in your entire body.

5. We're going to work on your face and nose. Scrunch up your nose as tight as you can, making lots of wrinkles in your face. Just keep scrunching. Now relax. Let's try it again; scrunch harder. Harder! Relax. Notice how relaxed your face feels.

6. Back to your tummy again. You're going to squeeze your belly as hard as you can, making you look as skinny as possible. Now squeeze . . . squeeze . . . squeeze. Good. You can relax now. Next, to try to make yourself even skinnier and hold it for a good five seconds each time. Squeeze. (Slowly count to five.) Relax. Let's try it one more time. Squeeze as hard as you can. (Count to five.) Relax. Now relax your entire body and notice how good that feels.

7. Now, pretend you're on a sandy beach. Use the muscles in your legs and squeeze your toes into the sand. Squeeze your toes into the sand as hard as you can. Feel the wet sand squish between your toes. Relax the muscles in your legs all the way down to your toes. Feel the tension wash away into the ocean. Let's try it again, only this time, dig your toes deeper into the sand, using your legs once again. Relax your legs. Relax your toes. Now, relax your entire body.

8. Pretend you're a rag doll, and let your entire body go limp. Notice how good it feels to be relaxed. Now, just enjoy the feeling. I am going to slowly count to three.

When I get to three, slowly open your eyes. One, two, three. Do you feel different than you did before we started? (Let the child answer.) Tell me what's different about how you feel now? (Let the child answer.) Now you know how to melt away the tightness in your body. Whenever you feel worried or upset or scared, take a few minutes to tighten your muscles, then relax them.

Let's Go to the Moon!

PURPOSE

To teach social skills, such as sharing, taking turns, and working together for children ages 4 through 10 in group therapy

MATERIALS

Paper and markers

Tell the children that we are all going on a trip to the moon. When we land, we will do a fun activity together.

Gather the children in a circle and have everyone sit. Count down from 10 until "blast off," when all the children should jump in the air.

Announce that we are now on the moon and we are going to make moon memories. Everyone will draw his or her own picture of the moon, while **sharing** the markers that are provided.

The only way for the group to get off the moon and go to home is to share. When one of the children doesn't share or snatches away a marker from another child, stop the activity and ask the children to talk about how it feels when someone takes something away from them.

You can also get creative here and design trips to other planet and lands to promote taking turns, saying please and thank you, and other manners and social skills.

FIRST and THEN Board

PURPOSE

To shepherd children ages 3 through 9 in completing non-preferred tasks in family or group settings. Kids often don't want to do activities that are required of them such as showering, going to bed, homework, etc. Use this activity to move those difficult moments along.

MATERIALS

Large poster board, scissors, a glue stick, card stock or a file folder, push pins or tape, pictures (photographs, pictures from magazines, images from Google images, cereal boxes, household supplies, wrappers, etc.)

A FIRST/THEN board can be used to communicate a sequence of events or to reinforce completion of a non-preferred activity. A first/then board can be used in a variety of ways:

- To assist with transition from one activity to another
- To assist in completing non-preferred tasks by reinforcing with a preferred activity
- Breaking a large schedule or sequence of events into smaller steps

First/Then board can be broken down into two-step activities, for example, "FIRST read a chapter; THEN use the computer."

You can also break down the FIRST into smaller steps, for example, "FIRST shirt, pants, socks, and THEN use the computer."

Making a FIRST/THEN Board

1. Gather the materials listed earlier. *Tip:* Every picture should have a label so the child can associate the written text with the picture.

2. Collect pictures to represent activities.

3. Cut the pictures out and paste them on card stock for durability or print on card stock.

5. Label top of the poster in two columns: FIRST/ THEN for each activity you are reinforcing.

Implementation

All FIRST activities are attached under the first column and all THEN activities are attached across from the FIRST activity.

My Happy Dance!

PURPOSE

To teach mindfulness and challenge negative thoughts, such as "I feel sad, but I choose to be happy," use the following activity with children during a session.

People who make me feel happy

_____

_____

Places I love to go to or I would like to visit

_____

_____

Things I love doing

_____

_____

Things that make me feel good

_____

_____

Brainstorm with the child or adolescent to answer the following questions, then create a list of pleasurable activities. When the child or adolescent feels sad or unhappy, encourage him or her to take out the list and read it.

Now You See It, Now You Do It

PURPOSE

To ease transitions that are difficult for children, particularly those aged 3 through 9, and can result in explosive behaviors and to reduce explosive behaviors and increase cooperation

Young children benefit from visual cues reminding them of what is next. Do the following, if possible, with the child:

1. Gather materials such as scissors, a glue stick, poster board, clear contact paper, pictures (photographs, pictures from magazines, images from Google, cereal boxes, household supplies, restaurant napkins, placemats, wrappers, etc.). Every picture should have a label so the child can associate the written text with the picture.

2. Choose pictures for the schedule you wish to create. Keep in mind that a visual schedule is used to assist children with transitions and anticipating activities throughout the day. It can be as specific or as general as the child may need and can be for varying spans of time. For example, a visual schedule may outline parts of a day, a half-day, or an entire day.

3. Cut your pictures and poster board squares the same size. Keep in mind your child's developmental level.*

4. Glue the pictures on poster board squares for durability.

5. Punch holes and string the pictures together with yarn or string in the order of the day.

6. Hang from a cabinet or hook at the top of a door.

Use the worksheet on page 74 with parents/caregivers to identify the transitions during the child's day.

Tip: Keep in mind the developmental stage of the child. Some children will understand what "getting dressed" means. Others will need a cue for each piece of clothing, such as images for shirt, underwear, pants, socks, and shoes.

WORKSHEET: NOW YOU SEE IT: TRANSITION PLANNER

List each transition in the child's day:

1. _____

2. _____

3. _____

4. _____

5. _____

6. _____

7. _____

8. _____

9. _____

10. _____

Now evaluate the following:

The child needs full supervision and prompting: yes or no

The child needs moderate supervision and prompting: yes or no

The child needs only the visual reminders: yes or no

Create a string of cues for each transition, keeping in mind developmental stages.

Up, Up, and Away

PURPOSE

To provide children ages 3 through 9 with a mindfulness exercise that will help their let go of problems, annoyances, and irritations; to help children to articulate problems that bother them; and to decrease meltdowns and tantrums.

Work with the child around the triggers that cause them to tantrum or meltdown and using the following as a guide.

1. Ask the child if he or she has ever had a problem that upset him or her, such as someone pushing to the front of the line, someone bumping into him or her—concentrate on easy to let go of problems.

2. Give the child an example: "I was waiting in line at the grocery store and the clerk shut the aisle down after I had already put my groceries down. I was so mad! I had to move all my food back into my cart and go to another line!"

3. Brainstorm with the child about things that bug him or her.

4. Have the child write each thing/problem on one of the hot air balloon (see the following page).

5. Say to the child, "Now let's imagine that the balloon is taking the problem way away into space, never to return."

Copy the worksheet on page 76 and give the child markers/crayons and have them write or draw pictures of problems on the balloon.

Tommy the Tiger: Narrative Story Telling

PURPOSE

To help children separate themselves from the problem through story telling

By constructing a story about a problem, children can experience themselves separate from the problem. This allows children to talk freely about what is going on, and they gain control over their feelings. Following is an example, addressing meltdowns at bedtime, of questions that can be asked to guide the child.

Therapist: "If the problem had a name what would it be?"

Child: "Tommy the Tiger."

Therapist: "It sounds like Tommy the Tiger shows up right at bedtime and keeps you from going to bed. How does Tommy the Tiger keep you from going to bed? Can you remember a time when Tommy the Tiger didn't show up at bedtime?"

Child: "He doesn't show up on Saturday night."

Therapist: "What is different about Saturday night?"

Child: "I don't know it's just different."

Therapist: "Tell me more about those times, what was different?

(The therapist continues to ask questions and comes up with the following: no homework, lots of time outside to run around, less structure, etc.)

Therapist: "What is the worst thing about it when Tommy the Tiger appears?"

Child: "Everyone is mad at me."

Therapist: "Tell me what would be like if Tommy the Tiger didn't visit you at bedtime anymore?"

Child: "Mommy and Daddy wouldn't be mad at me."

Therapist: "What else?"

Child: "I wouldn't be so tired in the morning."

Therapist: "Great, let's write a letter to Tommy the Tiger and ask him to stay at the zoo and not bother you at bedtime."

Use the worksheet on the following page to assist the child in writing their own letter.

Write the letter with the child and have him or her draw pictures.

Dear _____,

_____

_____

_____

_____

_____

_____

_____

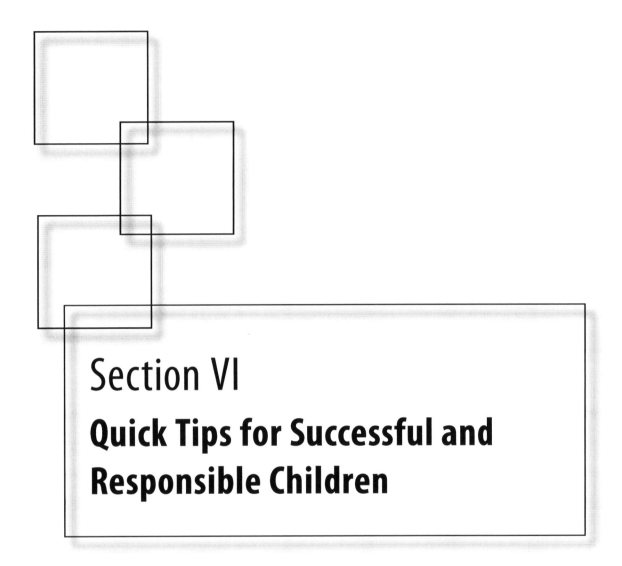

Section VI

Quick Tips for Successful and Responsible Children

You Are Your Child's Favorite Toy

PURPOSE

Teaching parents how to play with their children and increase their bond.

Invite parents/caregivers into the play therapy room and try these ideas:

- Remind parents that playing with kids doesn't have to be long and involved. It can be in 5- to 10-minute spurts.

- Have parent/caregiver read a short book or poem aloud to the child.

- Tell the parent/caregiver to ask the child, **"Can I play with you?"** In kid-speak, this means "I like you."

- Encourage adults to always approach children rather than having children approach adults for play. It always works out better if you don't have to say no because in kids-speak, it means "I don't like you."

- Sit with a child and watch him or her play without talking. Listen and watch—you will be surprised with the stories and information that they will share while playing.

  Draw on a piece of paper and cover up what you are doing. Kids are curious. They will pry your arm away to see, and when they do, you can ask, "Would you like a turn?"

I Am

PURPOSE

To increase feelings of self-worth in children who are depressed, worried, or anxious.

MATERIALS

Play dough or modeling clay, paper, and a pen

Brainstorm of positive attributes with the child, for example, "brave, a good friend, artistic, good speller, organized, etc."

I am _____.

I am _____.

I am _____.

I am _____.

I am _____.

Provide the child an assortment of different colors of clay.

Tell the child to pick one thing from the list and create an image out of the clay to represent it.

After the child makes the clay image, ask him or her, "Why did you choose that one? What can you tell me about it?"

Encourage the child to choose another attribute from the list and to do the exercise again. Have the child take the images home to reinforce positive thoughts and to increase his or her self-worth.

What Is Your Word?

PURPOSE

To encourage children and adolescents to find something meaningful to put at the center of their lives to overcome suffering and depression.

Keeping positive messages front and center gives us something to focus on to create success in our lives.

- Ask the child, "What is the one word that best describes you?" Answers could include "artist," "peacekeeper," "leader," "comedian," "computer whiz," and so on.

- Help the child or adolescent come up with a word that best describes a positive attribute that he or she has.

- Give the child or adolescent a piece of paper and have him or her draw, color, paint, and/or decorate that word so it is big and bold.

- Make five copies of this paper and send them home with the child or adolescent to hang in the bedroom, kitchen, bathroom, and so on, so that he or she sees this message multiple times a day.

Use the attribute list on page 89 to stimulate the conversation.

Positive Attributes List

Use this list to dig deeper and find more words that describe the child/adolescent in a positive light.

POSITIVE ATTRIBUTES LIST

adventurous	compassionate	enthusiastic
brave	conscientious	faithful
bright	considerate	friendly
calm	courteous	funny
careful	creative	generous
communicative	determined	gentle
loving	diligent	hardworking
loyal	easygoing	helpful
modest	patient	honest
neat	polite	kind
optimistic	reliable	thoughtful
sociable	sensible	warmhearted
sympathetic	sincere	

A Perfect Day!

PURPOSE

To mine for goals and dreams in adolescents (ages 13 through 18)

Have the adolescent spend a few minutes thinking about a perfect day would be like in his or her life. Encourage the adolescent write a story describing in detail everything about that day.

The following prompts will help the adolescent get started:

Where are you?

_____

_____

Who are you with?

_____

_____

What are you doing?

_____

_____

How do you feel?

_____

_____

Tweet Power

PURPOSE

To encourage teenagers (ages 13 through 18) to express themselves

Some teens aren't very conversational. This challenge will get them talking to you. Tell the teen, "On Twitter you only get 140 characters to express yourself. I will ask a question, and you respond by writing an answer using 140 characters." Allow them to use the computer with word application to count the characters. Use the worksheet on the next page for examples of questions.

WORKSHEET: TWEET POWER

Tell me something you accomplished in the last week.

_____

_____

_____

Tell me about something you did that you were proud of.

_____

_____

_____

If you could do anything in your life what would it be?

_____

_____

_____

If you could go anywhere where would you go?

_____

_____

_____

Are you an introvert or an extravert? Explain.

_____

_____

_____

What do you think that real friendship means?

_____

_____

_____

What do you think your life purpose is?

_____

_____

_____

Dear Best Friend (Responsible One)

PURPOSE

To encourage teens (ages 13–18) to be responsible by giving advice to others; this activity can be used in group therapy sessions.

By encouraging teens to give advice to their peers, they can often benefit by listening to someone else's problem. Also by distancing oneself from a problem, it is less threatening and easier to offer solutions.

- Instruct each member of the group to write a brief letter to someone he or she really trusts. The letter should consist of a request for advice concerning a real problem, present or past. In their letters, members should include enough facts and feelings so that the other group members will be able to relate.

- The letter should be signed with a made-up name.

- Collect the letters, and then pass them out again, ensuring that everyone will receive a letter that is not his or her letter.

- Instruct the group members to write a response to the letter they have.

- When the group finishes, have the group members read the letters and their responses aloud. Allow the group members to discuss the advice given, debating whether they agree or disagree and why? The therapist can also guide the process to reflect appropriate advice if need be.

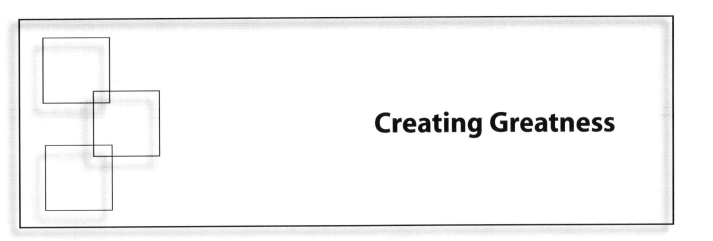

Creating Greatness

PURPOSE

To encourage teens to strive for greatness and success by examining others and themselves; this activity can be used in individual or group therapy sessions.

Exploring definitions of the words *average* and *exceptional* and exploring these behaviors with kids encourages them to strive for greatness.

Use the following worksheet, "Creating Greatness," to engage the teenager during the session. After the teen has filled out the worksheet, use this as a conversation starter.

WORKSHEET: CREATING GREATNESS

1. Write down the names of people you know that who are average achievers:
   (Average: usual or typical mediocre or inferior)

   _____

   _____

   _____

   _____

   _____

2. Write down three times in your life when your average achievements actually caused you to come up short:

   _____

   _____

   _____

   _____

   _____

3. Write down the names of people who you know are above average or exceptional and explain how they are different from "just average":

   _____

   _____

   _____

   _____

   _____

4. What's one small thing you can do going forward to be great or exceptional?
   (Exceptional: unusual; not typical)

   _____

   _____

   _____

   _____

The Dog Ate My Homework:
Excuses versus Reasons

PURPOSE

To help teens take responsibility for their actions and to help them move forward towards success.

Teens are quick to make excuses when they are ashamed or embarrassed. Encouraging them to take responsibility allows them to grow and learn from their mistakes. Use the following worksheet, "Excuses versus Reasons," with the teen during the session to begin a conversation and make this a teachable moment.

WORKSHEET: EXCUSES VERSUS REASONS

Share the following with the teen:

Excuses are never the reason why one does or doesn't do something. They are merely a revision of the facts construed to help one feel better about what did or did not happen. For example,

_____

_____

Excuse: You didn't turn your homework in because the dog ate it.

_____

_____

Reasons are the logical facts associated with a behavior. It forces personal responsibility where it is appropriate.

_____

_____

Reason: You didn't turn your homework in is because you left it where the dog could get it.

_____

_____

1. What are some of your favorite excuses?

_____

_____

2. What are the real reasons behind your excuses?

_____

_____

3. How do you feel when you use an excuse?

_____

_____

4. How does using an excuse keep you from being the best you, you can be?

_____

_____

Time, Time, Time

PURPOSE

To help teens identify how they spend their time, what the time wasters are, and how to make positive choices about what they are doing with their time

Encourage the teen to fill out the worksheets on pages 102 and 103 and then review it with them or the therapist can ask these questions and notate on the worksheet.

WORKSHEET: TIME, TIME, TIME

1. How much time are you at school each day?

   _____

   _____

2. How much time do you spend on homework?

   _____

   _____

3. How much time do you spend at meals?

   _____

   _____

4. How much time do you spend sleeping?

   _____

   _____

5. How much time do you spend doing some type of sport or activity?

   _____

   _____

6. How much time do you spend doing homework and seeking help for that homework?

   _____

   _____

7. How much time do you spend with friends doing something fun?

   _____

   _____

8. How much time do you spend on the Internet, playing video games, social media, texting, and so on?

   _____

   _____

9. How much time do you spend watching TV?

   _____

   _____

10. Of the activities you do, which do you think are time wasters?

   _____

   _____

Use this calendar to fill in what is happening now. And the second calendar how you would like it to look.

Sunday	Monday	Tuesday	Wednesday	Thursday	Friday	Saturday

Sunday	Monday	Tuesday	Wednesday	Thursday	Friday	Saturday

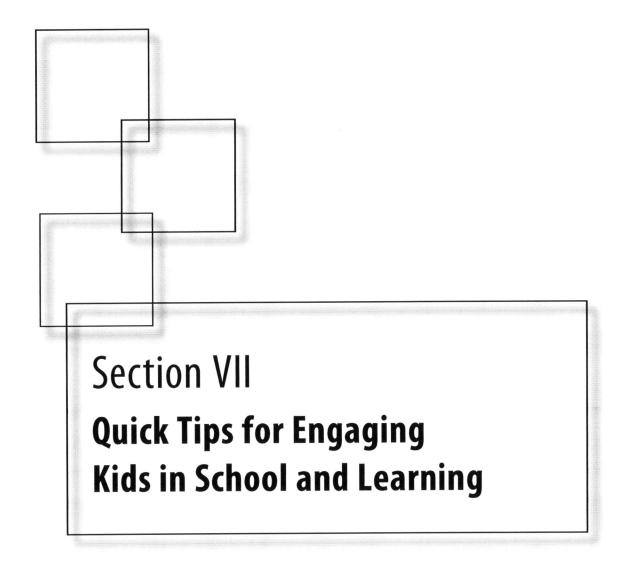

Section VII

Quick Tips for Engaging Kids in School and Learning

When Our Teens Don't Get Us and We Don't Get Them . . . and What to Do about It

Do you sometimes feel that you and your teenager live on different planets? Do you and your teen get frustrated and angry at each other? Do you notice that your take on a given situation is miles away from your teen's experience? If so, you are not alone. In fact, most parents of teenagers sometimes get mad at themselves for losing control and wonder what they can do about it. Sometimes the solution isn't what you think. Let me tell you how my son didn't get me and I didn't get him. I want you to know that we didn't just resolve this situation, I was also able to approach parenting in a whole new way from then on . . . and so will you.

Here is our story.

Parent Coach Susan Epstein's Real-Life Experience with her Two Teenagers

Mom's Point of View

A few summers ago, I was standing in the checkout line at the Gap with my two teenagers, Daniel and Sarah. We had just completed our yearly back-to-school shopping. With every item Dan had selected and had to have, he tossed it to me to carry. Now, I am a petite woman, I am 45 years old, and I had worked all day; it is 9 p.m. We have been in the mall since 6 p.m., and I was exhausted, irritable, weighted down, and broke. In one hand, I was holding two pair of pants, a sweatshirt, shirt, four pair of boxers, and a sweater. In my other hand was my purse and $250 of clothing that I purchased for Sarah at Old Navy.

There were three checkouts and four to five people in each line. It was a mob scene. I was almost there; I could already feel myself sinking into my bed and nodding off into dreamland. I was dead on my feet. I glanced up at the counter, and two of the checkout girls, not much older than my son, are giggling and discussing what they would be doing when they got off work that evening. I felt as if I have been in this line for 10 days, and I want to scream! Instead, I turned to my kids and said, in a whisper, "This is ridiculous!" Dan looks at me with disdain and hisses, "I hate it when people do that . . . it's soooooo rude!"

One of the girls looked up from behind the counter and sheepishly said, "I'll be right with you." I was instantly shamed. My more-than-truthful comment made me look like the "mom from hell" to the back-to-school shopping crowd.

Daniel's Point of View

We were at the gap. Mom was so cool; she was getting me whatever I want. I was going off to college and she felt bad. She liked everything I choose. I can't remember a better shopping spree with Mom. She was even carrying everything for me. We got everything I wanted in less than 30 minutes, and there was still plenty of time left to see my friends. It was awesome!

Now it was time to pay. We got in line. The line was really long. My cell phone rang, and it was one of my friends. We talked for a while, and then I told him that I'd pick him up real soon. I had taken my own car to the mall so I could split as soon as we were done.

My mom was breathing heavy and was looking really irritated and crabby. How can her moods change so quickly? All of a sudden she blurted out, really loudly, "This is ridiculous!" It was horrible; everyone in the store was looking at us. I tried to hide and to pretend that she was not my mom, so I said, "I hate it when people do that. It is soooooo rude!" Again, all eyes were looking at us, and I look away, again pretending I don't know her. Even the hot girl behind the counter knew how embarrassing it was to be out with your parents. She looked right at my mom and said, with an edge, "I'll be right with you." There, my mom was put in her place.

Now I feel bad: I want to be with my mom, but sometimes she can be such a dork!

Writing this experience from Daniel's perspective really helped me see where my son was coming from. We had different agendas: He had plans to go out with friends; I had plans to sleep. We had different energy levels: He had slept until noon; I had been up since 6 a.m. I was sad about him leaving for college the following week, and he couldn't wait to get to his dorm and meet his roommate. I showed Dan this piece after I wrote it, and we talked about how we sometimes see things from different angles. After this, I began to take a step back when I was confused about my teen's behavior. I thought about it from his point of view, and then I checked it out with him to see if I was on the right track.

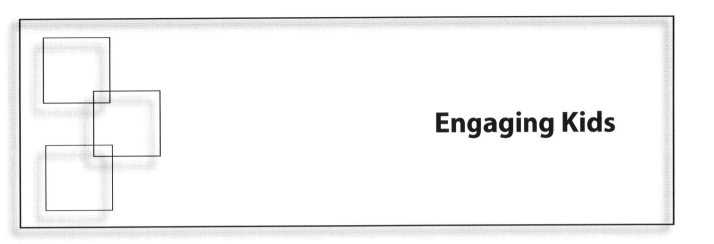

Engaging Kids

PURPOSE

To increase motivation in children and teens

The following are key components in kids being actively engaged in learning, conversation, and discovery. Use this checklist when looking at why a child or teen might be disengaged, bored, or disruptive in class or at home with homework. Answer yes or no to each.

The activity . . .

Y or N   activates prior knowledge.

Y or N   fosters active investigation.

Y or N   promotes group interaction.

Y or N   encourages collaboration.

Y or N   allows for choice.

Y or N   includes games and humor.

Y or N   supports mastery.

Y or N   nurtures independent thinking.

Y or N   does not make children wait.

The Most Amazing School Year

PURPOSE

To assist parents/caregivers in creating a new treatment plan.

Beginnings are a great time to look back and evaluate your expectations, goals, and aspirations. We learn from our mistakes, we learn from certain decisions and choices that seemed right at the time, and we learn, too, that even with the best intentions sometimes those choices led us down a rocky road.

Use the worksheet on the following page, "Three-Stage Plan for an Amazing School Year," to engage parents/caregivers in the child/teen treatment plan.

WORKSHEET: THREE-STAGE PLAN FOR AN AMAZING SCHOOL YEAR

Ask the parent/caregiver the following questions:

1. What was the best thing that happened last school year?

   _____

   _____

2. What was the worst thing that happened?

   _____

   _____

3. If you could do something over again, how would you handle it?

   _____

   _____

4. What advice would you give yourself for this new school year?

   _____

   _____

5. What do you know now that you wish you knew a year ago?

   _____

   _____

6. What are you concerns with your child today?

   _____

   _____

7. What are your dream, goal, and vision for this school year for your child?

   _____

   _____

Take **one thing** you want to improve or change, and break it down into three steps:

1. _____

   _____

   _____

2. _____

   _____

   _____

3. _____

   _____

   _____

I will complete these steps by _____.

"I Hate Homework!"

PURPOSE

To increase a student's engagement in homework and to eliminate power struggles, tantrums, and meltdowns

Parents and Teachers can encourage school engagement by creating and supporting assignments that have the following qualities.

Ask these questions before assigning homework or while looking over a homework assignment. Getting a yes to these questions will increase the student's willingness to complete the assignment and will increase engagement in learning:

- Does the student have a choice how he or she does the assignment?
- Does the student have a choice where he or she does the assignment?
- Does the student have a choice how much time it will take him or her to complete the assignment?
- Does the assignment engage the student in something new, or is it a regurgitation of something already taught in class?
- Does the student understand the *purpose* of the assignment?
- Does the assignment augment learning already begun in class?

My Special Project

PURPOSE

To promoting learning, excitement, and engagement in children and adolescents outside of the school environment and to increase self-esteem, confidence, creativity, motivation, and presentation skills. (This activity can be used in a group therapy format as well.)

Providing a creative learning environment at home is an exciting way to stimulate a child or teen's mind. Try this activity at home.

- Schedule a family meeting and tell the kids that everyone in the family is going to have a chance to create and showcase his or her own project. It can be whatever each kid wants.
- Brainstorm ideas such as designing a garden, creating a workspace in the basement, looking for rocks, and creating a presentation about something of interest. The ideas should be something the child or teen wants to do.
- Next, ask them what supplies they will need for their project and create a list.
- Gather the items together or shop for them if you don't have them.
- Pick a day—could be a Saturday, Sunday, or a vacation day—and mark it as PROJECT DAY on the calendar.
- Tell the kids they have from 8 a.m. until 4 p.m. (or whatever works) to design, create, and finish their project.
- After dinner (this night would be a fun night to get a pizza), have each family member stand up and show off his or her project.

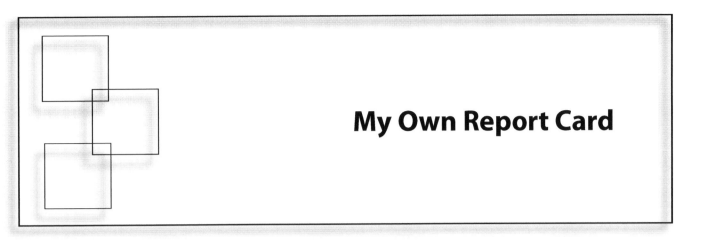

My Own Report Card

PURPOSE

To give kids useful and purposeful feedback on their school experience without associating it with a grade.

For children with attention deficit hyperactivity disorder, mental health issues, and/or learning disabilities, report cards can be demoralizing and hurtful. Oftentimes, grades do not reflect the effort that a student puts into his or her work.

At the beginning of the quarter or semester, ask kids for their top five learning goals. At the end of the quarter or semester, have the kids answer the following report card questions.

My Top Five Learning Goals:

1.

2.

3.

4.

5.

Use the worksheet on the following page with the child/teen to create their own report card that reflects effort, not grades.

WORKSHEET: MY OWN REPORT CARD

1. How did I do?

2. Did I succeed in learning what I set out to?

3. Do my grades reflect my effort?

4. What were my challenges?

5. What were my obstacles?

6. What did I excel at?

7. What needed more attention?

8. What did I love learning?

9. What bored me to tears?

10. What type of learning do I like the best: Watching? Listening? Doing?

The ME Poster

PURPOSE

To increase motivation, self-esteem, and sense of purpose for children and adolescents; this activity can be used in individual, group, family, home, and classroom therapy sessions.

Work with the child or adolescent to create a poster about themselves that shows them doing something they are proud of or that offers encouraging words.

Go to the Big Huge Labs website: bighugelabs.com/motivator.php

The following is a poster I created myself.

CARD BOARD BOAT RACE
You Can Do Anything When You Work As a Team

"Getting Unstuck" Cards

PURPOSE

To help kids move on from being overwhelmed, from suffering writer's block, or from obsessive thoughts; this activity can be used in individual, group, home, and classroom therapy settings.

MATERIALS

Card stock or 3 × 5 cards and an assortment of colored markers

Brainstorm to create statements, questions, or prompts to light that fire for the child or teen. Tell the child or teen to create a stack of at least 10 cards to use when he or she is stuck.

The following are examples of prompts:

What would my best friend do?

Look away and then look at it again.

What am I resisting?

What is needed?

What are other possibilities?

Where do I limit myself?

If I were at my best, what would I do now?

What is it to be focused?

Get Unstuck

Get Unstuck

Get Unstuck

Section VIII

Quick Tips for a Happy, Healthy Home

One Perfect Moment

Most parents and educators dream of one perfect day with the kids, one day during which there was no hitting, kicking, screaming and no "You can't make me!" Homework is completed without nagging; teeth are brushed without reminding; dinnertime is filled with wonderful conversations; and when you tuck your angels into bed there are many smiles—like on *Leave it to Beaver* and *The Brady Bunch*.

Oh, to all be so happy and relaxed! I remember wishing for this many times. As I look back on the last 10 years, when I was raising my kids, a portion of which I was a single parent, I don't think that there ever was one perfect day.

I am quite amazed that I could do it all: working full-time, dinner on the table six of seven nights, lunches made, cookies baked, homework, bath time, reading to the kids, doctors and dentist appointments, shopping, cleaning, Little League, dance, Girl Scouts, selling cookies and wrapping paper, religious school, birthday parties, school plays, chicken pox, stomach flu, strep, up all night with sick kids, friends for the kids, sledding, ice skating, swimming lessons, holiday shopping, holidays in general, snow days, planning summers, planning and making vacations happen, finding sitters, making time for me and my interests, taking care of me (exercising, eating well, etc.), and being totally, totally, flexible!

What I did have were many, many perfect moments, and these are the moments I cherished then and remember today. How would you like more perfect moments? I am going to share my secret:

- Time is a commodity: I planned, planned, and planned.

- We shut off the TV Sunday night through Thursday nights (more time together, no arguing about what to watch or when to go to bed).

- I had a sitter, a backup sitter, and another backup sitter.

- I traded with other moms and dads for free time.

- I cooked on Sundays for the whole week.

- I made all lunches on Sundays.

- I learned to say no to a lot of people.

- I did not involve my kids in more than two after-school activities each week (preferably just one).

- Piano lessons were given at our house (no driving and waiting).

- We had a basketball hoop at our house (I knew where the kids were).

- We had family time, games, puzzles, and laughter.

- And when I felt overwhelmed, I asked for help from friends, relatives, and experts.

Obesity and Depression: The New Childhood Disease

Overweight children, compared to children with a healthy weight, suffer from social discrimination and low self-esteem. Depression in children and adolescents can be the cause and the consequence of obesity. In fact, some kids who are overweight have a higher level of anxiety than do other children.

The fallout from this includes:

- teasing at school and through social media;
- difficulties playing sports, which compounds the problem;
- fatigue, which contributes to depression; and
- sleep apnea, which contributes to poor sleep and thus a shorter fuse.

Our hearts break for these kids, and we oftentimes don't know how to help.

What we do to help?

- Have a medical evaluation completed first to rule out a physical cause.
- Emphasize healthy eating—clean out your cabinets together and read the labels.
- Create awareness by making three piles on the kitchen table: foods to keep, foods to never buy again, and foods to throw away (look for sugar and other unhealthy additives).
- Let the child know he or she is loved and appreciated.
- If you suffer from overweight or obesity yourself, create a family goal to get healthy.
- Shop together for fruits, vegetables, and lean protein.
- Plan meals and cook together.
- Take walks together and plan active outings.
- Be a role model for your child so he or she has someone to look up to and admire.

Time Away from the Kids

Are you are so busy, striving for a clean house and home-cooked meals? For exercising daily, eating right, watching your weight, having rewarding employment, having a social life and fulfillment? For being the best mom or dad you can be?

Do you feel something is missing? Are you noticing that

- you and your partner don't spend time together?

- you and your partner are arguing with no resolution?

- you feel that you are letting him or her down?

- you want to add more intimacy and romance in your life?

- you and your partner have a dream, such as going on vacation, and you don't know how to make that happen?

- you have an issue that is causing stress in your relationship (e.g., kid issues, job issues, troubles with infertility, or your relationship with in-laws)?

- you are going through a life transition, such as a new job, a baby, a new romance, a new marriage, your kids growing up and leaving home, having to care for an elderly parent?

Is it time to start paying attention to your relationship with your partner? "But Susan, we both work full-time, and the kids demand all of our attention!" Paying attention to your relationship will put you both at the top of the list, and when you nurture and support each other, everything else will seem much more manageable.

Steps for Caring for Each Other

- Get a babysitter if you need to and go out one time a week. Pick a night and stick to it. It doesn't have to be Saturday! It doesn't matter what you do—you can even go food shopping together. Just make it alone time.

- Make a specific time each evening as "off duty." For example, tell the kids, "Bedtime is 8:30p.m., and we are now on break; no interruptions." Follow through to ensure you and your partner have at least an hour alone each evening.

- Explore activities and hobbies that you have in common. As your kids get older, begin to do these activities together, such as, for example, running, tennis, dancing, skiing, photography, or hiking.

- Talk about intimacy and schedule time to be alone and reconnect. Notice when your partner does something kind and comment to him or her about it.

- Get conscious in your relationship and pay attention to what is going on.

These steps are not automatic, and they take planning and organization. But the work is well worth it in the end. But just a little caveat, some days the laundry just won't get folded, and there might be some dishes in the sink when you wake up in the morning, but sometimes, letting go of some mundane tasks will be well worth it!

Messy Home, Messy Mind

"If a home doesn't make sense, nothing does."
– Henrietta Ripperger

I just came across this quote, and it made me stop and think how true this is; messy rooms, dirty dishes, chaos in our junk draws, and unplanned meals can certainly have a major impact on each day of our lives. I know for me, that if I don't have some order my mind feels messy, too. It made me think about all the systems that I have created over the years and about how implementing those systems in my life while my kids were growing up provided me with a clear mind and wonderful memories. We didn't fight about messy rooms, money, curfews, and homework because I had a system for each of those. Consider implementing the following for a healthy home and healthy mind:

- Regular shopping trips
- Regular bedtimes
- Regular mealtimes
- Regular cleaning days
- Regular laundry days
- Menus for the week
- Schedules for watching TV
- Allowances
- Homework time

The key is "regularity" and "schedules"! These provided my kids and me the structure we needed for our busy, full, productive lives.

Pay the Jar

PURPOSE

To reduce sibling conflict, hitting, kicking, and name-calling, among other unwanted behaviors

When my children were five and nine, they were constantly calling each other names and hitting each other. Sound familiar? Well, it drove me bananas, and I knew I had to nip it in the bud!

So I created a fine system:

     25 cents for a name

     50 cents for a smack

I put a label on a jar that said "FINES."

I gave them each 2 dollars in change at the beginning of the week. If they called each other names or hit each other, I would make them "pay the jar."

The first week, I collected a lot of change, and I would tease them, saying, "Mommy's getting rich!"

They quickly figured out that if they kept their language "appropriate" and kept their hands and feet to themselves, they could keep their change. The bad habits were cured within two weeks.

Then I implemented the "Allowance Is What You Are Allowed" Plan, which continued the lesson, teaching them how to plan and save and spend wisely. (See *Title of Piece*, vol. 1, "Allowance").

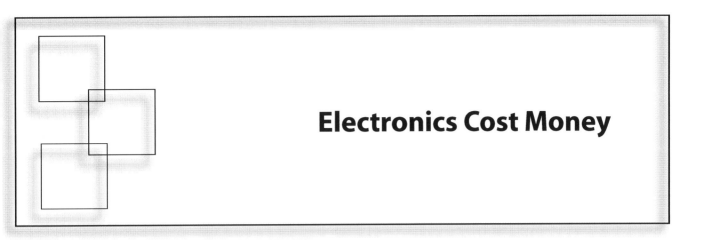

Electronics Cost Money

PURPOSE

To teaching financial responsibility and for controlling use of electronics at home

MATERIALS

Jar or container and quarters

Because you are paying the bills for all things "electronic," explain to the kids that they will have to pay to use these things as well. Each child will be given a set amount of coins at the beginning of the week that he or she must allocate for using the electronics. When the money runs out, that's it for the week.

You can offer an incentive that if there is leftover money at the end of the week, he or she can spend it at the grocery store on a special treat when you go shopping.

First, determine how much of each electronic you would approve of on average per week. If your child is permitted to watch one hour of TV and to use the computer for one hour of computer time a day, multiply that times 7, for a total of 14 hours of total electronics per week. If every hour costs 50 cents, then that is a total of 7 dollars per week.

Consider breaking down the available time into 30-minute intervals and providing quarters for payment.

Rainy Day Tool Kit (Expressive Arts for Creative Minds)

Well, it is cold, real cold, and rainy—the kind of day during which you don't want to leave the house. But you know if you don't get out, by the end of the day, your nerves are going to be frayed (from your children's fighting and bickering, from their nagging you, from your nagging them), and the kids will have probably lost every toy and privilege under the sun. Those long, sad faces will be looking at you for the rest of the day.

You have probably tried letting them watch TV for hours, but after a while, as you watch them turn into zombies in front of your very eyes, the guilt gets to you. On one hand, you realize that sitting in front of a talking box just isn't healthy; however, you are out of ideas about what to do. Why can't they just play alone, or together, or just occupy themselves? I'll tell you why.

The kids are out of ideas, just like you are. They are accustomed to using TV, video games, and time on computer as their wind-down activity. Very rarely do our kids have a whole day of nothingness stretching out before them.

- They need you to provide structure and ideas.
- They need you to spark their creative minds.
- They need you to turn off the TV so they can think and learn and build.

The following are some creative ideas you can pull together in no time with items found around your home or classroom.

Make Play Dough

Get out the cookie cutters and let the kids make a mess. Once it dries, it is a breeze to clean up.

Here are a few fun to make recipes!

Play Dough

2 cups flour

3 tbsp cream of tartar

1/2 cup salt

4 tbsp oil

1/2 cup boiling water

food coloring

Mix dry ingredients together. Mix oil, food coloring, and boiling water in a separate container. Stir liquid mixture until cool enough to knead. Knead until smooth. If the play dough is too dry, add more water, a little at a time. If play dough is too crumbly, knead in a small amount of oil. Store in an airtight container.

No-Cook Play Dough

4 cups flour

1 cup salt

4 tbsp oil

1 1/2 cup water

Mix oil and food color together before adding to dry mixture. Mix until pliable. Keep in container or plastic bag.

More Ideas!

Make a Treasure Chest

Shoeboxes, magazines, and glue sticks are all that is needed to make great art projects. Let kids decorate the boxes and then use them for storing their treasures.

Family Photo Gallery

Go through photographs. Let the kids cut them up and make a collage from the photos from a family vacation.

Let's Play School

Set up a schoolroom and let the kids be the teachers to each other.

Let's Find It!

Have an indoor scavenger hunt.

Picnic

Have a picnic lunch in the family room; sit on beach towels and eat in your bathing suits to mix things up.

Fort!

Let the kids build a fort out of chairs and blankets.

Performance

Give your kids a bag of objects and have them put on a skit for you using the objects.

Sit back and watch your kids have fun while knowing that you are sparking their creative minds!

The Creative Brain

PURPOSE

To teach children to play on their own without the use of electronics and to encourage creativity and brain function

MATERIALS

A paper bag or shoebox, stickers, markers, magazines, scissors, glue sticks, timer, and index cards

Whether you do this as part of a therapy session or as a parent/child activity, work together to create dozens of ideas that encourage hands on, creative activities that stimulate the mind.

1. Provide children with the materials above and ask them to decorate a bag or box.

2. Using the worksheet, brainstorm with the child at least 25 activities that they can do alone that are not electronic (no TV, phone, iPad, iPod, etc.)

3. Set the timer for one minute and have the children call out ideas as fast as they can while taking turns. Get silly! Make it fun!

4. Transfer the best ideas onto the index cards either with images of that activity or with the activity name written out.

   Put the completed index cards into the box or bag, and the next time the child says, "I'm bored," "I have nothing to do," or "Can I use the computer or watch TV?" point him or her to his or her box or bag and say, "You have so much you can do!"

Parents/caregivers, use the worksheet on the following page to begin the brainstorm with the child. Then use the card worksheet to transfer the best ideas.

WORKSHEET: THE CREATIVE BRAIN

Fun Stuff I Can Do Alone or with a Friend

1. _____
2. _____
3. _____
4. _____
5. _____
6. _____
7. _____
8. _____
9. _____
10. _____
11. _____
12. _____
13. _____
14. _____
15. _____
16. _____
17. _____
18. _____
19. _____
20. _____
21. _____
22. _____
23. _____
24. _____
25. _____

Creative Brain Activity

Creative Brain Activity

Creative Brain Activity

Does Your Life Have Rhythm?

Think about the world: day and night; the seasons; the tides going in and out; the days, months, and years. We are given an order by which we live. How do you use this? Do you have regular bedtimes, mealtimes, relaxation breaks, workdays, and exercise and movement times? Or are your days spent reacting to chaos and fires to which you are continually reacting?

If the latter is the case, you are most likely depleted by the end of the day. Structure helps us keep our energy even and plentiful. Chaos leads to disorganization, poor sleep, poor eating habits, and anxiety, and our relationships suffer.

What if your days and nights were built on a structure that was easy and fun to implement? Would you want to do this?

The following suggestions are ones I have used over the years to help me streamline my life and leave time for the stuff that really matters to me:

- **When you prepare a dinner, multiply the recipe at least times two.** Freeze the unused portions and label them with a date. This gives you a no-cook night. Once you've got the hang of it, you'll only have to cook a couple of times a week because you'll always have something healthy and tasty that you can defrost, heat up, and serve. (Yippeee! More time relaxing, spending time with those you love!)
- **Pick a time of day for movement.** Put it on your calendar. Do different things each day such as go up and down the stairs 10 times, take a short walk around the block, do four of your favorite yoga poses, stand at your desk while working, and so on. (Yippee! Even if you don't make it to the gym, you still moved!)
- **Pick a bedtime that allows you a minimum of seven hours of sleep. (I plan on nine!)** Thirty minutes before bed, turn off the TV; put the laptop, iPad, and phone away; and read a book or a magazine.

Rhythm has a lot to do with planning. Life happens and things get messy, such as when a hurricane, a blizzard, or an earthquake occurs. Then all settles down and it's back to the ebb and flow of life.

Free Time? What's That?
Taking Care of You

Whether you are a parent or a professional or both, it is essential that you recharge your own batteries. Throughout this book, I have stressed being "on" with your kids and not allowing their negative behaviors to go unnoticed. I also realize that you require downtime and grown-up time.

Making time for yourself while raising kids and/or working with kids can be a huge challenge. In fact, it may feel like likes an impossibility given your job, long commute, household chores, kids' activities, busing the kids to and from, laundry, meal prep, shopping, cleaning—tired yet?

So where do you fit it eating right, exercising, socializing, alone time, reflection, fun, or just plain doing nothing?

Today, I want you to do some research; that means keep track of what you do and when you do it.

Notice the following things:

- **How many times you check your e-mail, your phone, social networking sites, and so on**
- Are distracted from what you are doing and not complete tasks, only to have to come back to it later and restart
- How often you wing it without planning and create extra work for yourself
- Your bedtime routines and your mealtime routines

Use the following worksheet to identify the daily activities that are time wasters.

After you do this fill in the activities you want to make time for.

All of this will save you precious time and create space for you to do nothing, or read a book, or put your feet up.

WORKSHEET: CREATING TIME FOR ME

Activities that are time wasters:

1. _____

_____

2. _____

_____

3. _____

_____

4. _____

_____

5. _____

_____

Activities that I want to fit in:

1. _____

_____

2. _____

_____

3. _____

_____

4. _____

_____

5. _____

_____

Splish, Splash: Seizing Opportunities of Joy and Connection

Last fall, I pulled up to the dry cleaners to drop off a few winter coats. It was a damp day; the rain had stopped, but the aftermath of the storm had left the parking lot full of puddles. I sat in car for a few minutes before getting out, watching a dad with his two-year-old boy navigate the lot with a big basket of laundry on their way to the Laundromat next to the dry cleaners.

Dad carried the laundry, and the two-year-old had a small bag, too. At the edge of the sidewalk was a puddle. His dad's back was to him, and the little boy walked right through it. He turned around and a glorious smile appeared on his face.

He turned around to check where his dad was—his dad was still walking—and then the little boy jumped back in the puddle and stamped his feet. His smile got bigger; the child's joy was classic. Next he got up onto the sidewalk—by now, his dad was struggling with the door to the Laundromat—and the little boy went back to the puddle for yet another jump.

At this moment, his dad saw him. A look of anger, frustration, now crossed his dad's face, and he grabbed the little boy's arm and dragged him into the Laundromat.

This made me sad. I thought of all the missed opportunities that busy, stressed-out parents, caregivers, and professionals give up for the "have-to-dos."

The next time you see a puddle, I challenge you to get in there with the child or teen in your life. It doesn't have to be a literal puddle, but the opportunity to stop, watch, and join the absolute joy that splashing together can provide.

References/Resources

Bronson, P and A. Merryman. 2009. *NurtureShock, New Thinking about Children*. Twelve: Hachette Book Group.

Bradbury T. and J. Greaves 2009. Emotional Intelligence 2.0. TalentSmart; Har/Dol En edition

Cardone, G. 2011 The 10X Rule: The Only Difference Between Success and Failure. Wiley

Epstein, Susan P. 2012. Over 60 Techniques, Activities & Worksheets for Challenging Children and Adolescents. Premier Publishing & Media

Freeman, J., Epston, D. & Lobovits, D. (1997) Stories of hope. In Playful Approaches to Serious Problems: Narrative Therapy with Children and Their Families. New York: Norton.

Godin, Seth. 2011. *We are all Weird*. The Domino Project

Hall, Kevin. 2009. Aspire: Discovering Your Purpose Through the Power of Words. William Morrow

James, B. 1989. Treating Traumatized Children: New Insights and creative interventions. New York: The Free Press

Lowndes, L. 2003. How to Talk to Anyone: 92 Little Tricks for Big Success in Relationships. McGraw Hill

Parry, A. & Doan, R.E. 1994. Stories Re-visions: Narrative Therapy in Postmodern World. New York: Guilford Press.

Pink, Daniel H. 2005. A Whole New Mind. Allen & Unwin

Pink, Daniel H. 2009. *Drive*. River Head Books.

Whitworth, L. & Kimsey-House, H., Sandahl, P. 1998. *Co-Active Coaching*. Davies-Black Publishing.

WEBSITES

www.ParentingPowers.com (Susan P. Epstein, LCSW, Free Special Report, free parenting tips, videos, tele-classes & Parenting Community.

www.GetHealthyWithSusan.com (Susan's Health Coaching site)

http://www.childhealthpolicy.sfu.ca/research_quarterly_08/rq-pdf/RQ-1-10-Winter.pdf

> For your convenience, we have established a dedicated website to download all the worksheets and exercises. This gives you a choice to photocopy from the book or print them.
>
> **go.pesi.com/techniques**

Made in the USA
Lexington, KY
28 October 2014